"What use are poets in a dark time?", wrote Hölderlin. Steve Light's ultra-compressed poetry tempers and disciplines his fertile and torrential imaginaire under the sign of Paul Celan, a potent influence. *Against Middle Passages* requires, in Light's phrase, "the trace's perseverance", so that we may "stand guard over absent meaning" (Blanchot) in our daily lives. The fragmentary insights of lyric flare briefly but intensely in a dark time.

ANTHONY RUDOLF,
AUTHOR OF *EUROPEAN HOURS* AND *SILENT CONVERSATIONS*

This indefatigable light errant draws us into the maelstrom of this aphoristic work with the understated stance that the title announces. Hyphen is the cleave by which these leaves move to replace the logic and practice of Middle Passage before we are trumped by the backwardness of our species. From the "soma-bog" of mercantilism to the bark of Birkenau we face our baseness. Recommended tempos: *larghissimo* at first pass, then *andante*...

ROBERT HARVEY, DISTINGUISHED PROFESSOR, STONY BROOK UNIVERSITY AND AUTHOR OF *WITNESSNESS: BECKETT, DANTE, LEVI AND THE FOUNDATIONS OF RESPONSIBILITY* (CONTINUUM/BLOOMSBURY, 2010) AND *SHARING COMMON GROUND: A SPACE FOR ETHICS* (BLOOMSBURY, 2017)

Poetry at its best! Outgrowths of nature and words intertwine with the verbal precision of haiku minimalism.

> DALIA JUDOVITZ, NEH PROFESSOR OF FRENCH, EMORY UNIVERSITY. AUTHOR MOST RECENTLY OF *GEORGES DE LA TOUR AND THE ENIGMA OF THE VISIBLE*

These are chiseled, lapidary poems of a gently expansive concentration, a discontinuous continuum of riff-like, free-falling interjections.

> HOWARD EILAND, CRITIC AND TRANSLATOR: CO-AUTHOR OF *WALTER BENJAMIN: A CRITICAL LIFE* AND TRANSLATOR OF *WALTER BENJAMIN: THE ARCADES PROJECT*

The expression "middle passage" evokes the crossing of the Atlantic Ocean which was necessary to convey black slaves from Africa to America. By juxtaposing "against" to this tag, Steve Light's text seeks to organize a response to the heinous political and commercial enterprises which punctuate our past, recent, and contemporary histories featuring genocides and ecocides. To voice this momentous "against", the book effectively deploys techniques miming struggle and disarticulation and skillfully involves the diligent reader's activity within the phenomenology of metaphorical resistance. Multiple short fragments, each adrift on the page it anchors in a singular geography, arrest our advance and foreground our sense of aporia or "not-passage." While their paratactic assemblage denies us a facile recuperation, these reefs bloom with particular corals, a dazzling vegetation of poetic resources which demonstrate a will to survive wreckage and dare us to address the ineffable, the ending.

    MARC-ANDRE WIESMANN,
    EMERITUS PROFESSOR OF FRENCH AND THE HUMANITIES
    SKIDMORE COLLEGE

Against Middle Passages

Steve Light

SPUYTEN DUYVIL
New York City

Some of these poems previously appeared in *Aufgabe*, *Poetry East*, *Rainbow Curve: A Journal of Contemporary Literature*, *Rattapallax: A Journal of Contemporary Literature*, *Rivet: Writing that Risks*, and *Yefief: A Journal of Art and Literature*.

©2018 Steve Light
ISBN 978-1-944682-87-3
Cover: Naoko Haruta, Life #133: 'Africa #4', acrylic on canvas, 43" x 67"
Image courtesy of the artist

Library of Congress Cataloging-in-Publication Data

Names: Light, Steve, 1961- author.
Title: Against middle passages / Steve Light.
Description: New York City : Spuyten Duyvil, [2018]
Identifiers: LCCN 2017037008 | ISBN 9781944682873
Classification: LCC PS3612.I3447 A6 2018 | DDC 811/.6--dc23
LC record available at https://lccn.loc.gov/2017037008

*for my parents, Fred and Edith,
whose courage and steadfastness in the struggle for social,
racial, economic, and political justice, ever and always
resonate within me as a sustaining and beneficent force
and whose personal goodness, sweetness, generosity, and wisdom
will always be my greatest and most beautiful fortune*

...the world's course from and through the Middle Passages to all the other annihilations and disappearances of our modernity, of the First Nations in the Caribbean and in the entirety of the hemisphere and once again of our 20th/21st Century modernity—Congolese, Herero and Nama, Armenian, Ukrainian, Jewish, Vietnamese, Indonesian, Timorese, Cambodian, Tutsi, Congolese again and everywhere and everyone else....in and amidst our contemporaneity: of the Disappeared and Perished....

distance-cored
to the leaving, leaved,
to bark, the tide-barred banks
to the wintered,
to the tide-cloistered rains,
moored to the sign-barred,
to the oar-weighted,
the oar-wracked writhing

spill,
world,
pain word
pain-ward
clustered

bespeeched,
star-sap
in the iris-nova

borecindered,
stayed-cipher,
to the name-sundered
borne

bale
the dark
racked
to the stammered name

welled
in the none-noun,
scoop-char in the time-welt

mass-
acred
to the acres and acres

light scrambles from the breach
in a circle of effortless pain
star-spore in the fever of expiration
a stammer of hands
in the shapeless surprise
the swift nearness gives way

flowers shivering
against windows

the restless plovers
filter in their flight
their sparse abode
their lost concordance,
tocsin of the merciless chill
at the river's mouth

toward-
less, proximate-less,
wintered-fired
promise-blotted

take as if from the mirror
the last wisp
the last mote
as if from the last star
bound in a web of glass

a rise in the naught,
in the embacled,
scrawl-wide, mneme-rent

each sun
in the transient eternity
of the light's remorse

thread stars in a name
in a name thread the leaves

heaped,
as,

toward the leaves
toward the leaves
keel-raced,
hand over hand
in the gauntlet of light

leaved,
leafed,
bereft

my ardor
touches my anguish
like water a tree's root

cleaveless,
reachlessly

tilled in the turning,
to the tilling told
in the root-ground,
stemmed to turning, staved,
against the bark
in the stemmed light unthreaded

what can abound
ranged to naught in the eyes'
brief squander?
pebbles through the water
thorn-sewn to the rimless fever
light-brimmed,
abyss-strayed
in the hand-spanned breach

linger so the rain
might linger too
as though
each instant
knew each moment

starred
to the billowing scale
of eyes

thirst of the sand
when the desert
wind dies

leaf to splint
and sun
peels pain
the shaken
dirge of stony water

torrential memory
in each

leaven-stilled spore,
oar stilled
nor want
nor word
to the friable waters

swarm-rhyme
in the bright,
pane-shattered beneath
the scurry of wings
maze of black leaves in the fountain
burdened in astral occasion

**light-blister,
semblance-smoke**

do we speak immensely
in the swift ellipsis?
the sovereign waters
in the plumbless well

my lips upon
the light
upon the fathoms
of your eyes

circle in the grain,
in-grained
in the light's sole
apostrophe

thrown
to rails,
rail-told,
rain-barred

seed-trialed
sun-spawn
stun-stammered

sown beneath
the leaves

hands to the rain-sung
scribelessly
the shore-distanced leap
lest-sentienced

lips to the leaves,
to the rain,
root-scathed
in the unloomed
unloamed light

anguish shadows,
horizon crests

stain-worded stencil
of this nearly
to lips, frost-rimed
star woven to the melting glass

towardlessly,
inunnumbered

barb-nova,
the light-torn
breath

gesticulate,
source-mime
tideshred
shellshard

the wrested
waters keel
in the circle's summons

each breath
in the steeped light
of each promise

bloomed in the quarry
of branches
suns to tides
surfaced in the shell-sown weight

siege-stemmed
voice-bright

im-palmed
in the pain
wrapped

shore leaf,
branch-tear,
oar-torn

none-,
none-such,
none-harvest

fount to the pore-gained,
to the swift steps

a tattered sleeve
hangs in the air caught
on a windowless ledge
pennon of wasps
emblem of the tattered sky

whelmed
in the murmur-seething
in the murmur-swelter

versed,
wound-rhyme

in the one ration-
speck

trammel
weft-ravage,
rode-cambered
song

sight-cry,
wisp-cry

soma-bog,
in each, in every,
each endlessly

leaves blemish
in the snow

nor frost convey
the purpose
of the light

fallow stone,
to sap,
leap-tide,
horizon-densed

yet still
flower

light-mask,
to the well
marsh water
in the pebble's path

to count
all the names

a mirror dipped
in the stream

mute-rime,
sundered array

un-anchored
ache

core-pebbled
to graft-wearied shoots
upon penultimate slopes

we bruise
in the irrevocable
breach

in the scar-cymbaled
spore wrought

further
to none
to no-one

world-temblor
in the voice-famish

nothing invents us
star-stria
in the tide-torment

torrent-coiffed
stammer-reached
in the eye-signed

errant light
in the embrace
rendered

each breath
drawn through each mote
through each
grain of sand

the light frays,
in grief condensed

in the dusk-ruddered
roar the fled-swum

glance-song
throe tide
in the scribed sun
horizon in the gamut-trace

quickened distance
in the scansion replied

Wstawac

do not sleep
lie still
and never close your eyes
one blink
and dawn shall be
upon you

fled to the rim
world-height
in the light-braised well

hands clutched
through a snowbank

no dreams
of the summer rain

can the world
still bleed
from its pneumatic scar

swift-marrow,
leavened in the nimb-pebbled
mesh-bright, mesh-bruised,
stamen-song

what
the depth does
not know
what
the knowing
does not deepen

clamor of each root
crumbling
hand to word
to ward the damaged
distance from

sail to dye-stained hands
breath-strafe
cratered
ward-less

if life
were light lost
light gone astray
in the star-nova's grief

the river's swift reflection
the broken cleft
of broken branches

leaf-struck to the light's
stemmed rupture
the tide-molted rush
maze-hurtled in the grief marrow

hide the leaves
between pages
the words
between leaves

rain-wall
cinder-splay

like lips
like eyes
to the frozen windows

water scars
the sands

the flight of marsh birds founders
in the root-mimed distance

burrow in the word
across the stricken shore

the trace's perseverance

each color borne
to its own mortal invention

a rehearsal of leaves
in the windless

hoarfrost
at summer's extremity

in the stiched wounds
of a child's hands
the last threads
of the world

verblessly
stumbled

ur-phoneme
of the tide-weight

the savanna's noon-day stones
exude their brave fervor
like the savanna's stars
their indefatigable light

how the root rears back
in the light's long uproar
carried in the one promise
leaf-massed

"...*I always think [she/he] will return, always,
whenever I see someone coming towards me....*"
–A Mother of *the Disappeared*–

and all of dawn
gathered in her eyes
and songbirds drift in the clear
and in the light

STEVE LIGHT is a poet and philosopher. He is the translator of Jean Grenier's *Islands: Lyrical Essays* and his translations of poems (and in instances essays) by the Italian poets Pasolini, Solmi, Ungaretti, Quasimodo, Saba, and Carraba, the French poets Jean-Baptiste Para and Alain Suied, as well as Rilke, Mandelstam, Tsvetaeva, and Pasternak have appeared in the U.S., Canada, and the U.K. His own writings have appeared in the U.S., Canada, Jamaica, the U.K., Australia, France, Italy, Japan, Russia, Spain, Germany, China, Kenya, Argentina, and Brazil.

www.ingramcontent.com/pod-product-compliance
Lightning Source LLC
Chambersburg PA
CBHW012101090526
44592CB00017B/2643